empty

making(?)

in a word

Blessings!
Heidi

joy

forgiveness

sleep

prayer

peace

in a word *

*quiet little thoughts about God

HEIDI FLOYD

CONCORDIA PUBLISHING HOUSE · SAINT LOUIS

Published by Concordia Publishing House
3558 S. Jefferson Avenue, St. Louis, MO 63118-3968
1-800-325-3040 · www.cph.org

Text © 2011 Heidi Floyd

Written by Heidi Floyd

Library of Congress Cataloging-in-Publication Data

Floyd, Heidi.
  In a word : quiet little thoughts about God / Heidi Floyd.
    p. cm.
  ISBN 978-0-7586-2727-8
  1. Christian women--Prayers and devotions. I. Title.
  BV4844.F63 2011
  242'.643--dc22
                                              2011015172

Manufactured in the United States of America

1 2 3 4 5 6 7 8 9 10   20 19 18 17 16 15 14 13 12 11

to my family—

For those I get to kiss every day,
for those I don't get to see as much as I'd like,
and for those I won't hug again until
I am called home. You make my heart happy.

FOREWORD

Heidi Floyd tells some pretty remarkable stories. Stories of hope, inspiration, and life. Then again, Heidi's own story is pretty remarkable.

When I first met her, Heidi's husband, Stuart, was a seminary student. She had just gone to the doctor and received the good news that she was pregnant. Shortly thereafter, she received news that was not so good. Heidi had been diagnosed with cancer, and her prospects looked grim. The doctor advised her that she had a tough road ahead of her. The chemotherapy was sure to make her weak. For the sake of her health, the doctor advised her to have an abortion. If she had done so, who could have blamed her? Her life was on the line. She was already a wife and a mother of three daughters. She had responsibilities. Perhaps, another child later, but not now. But, no, that's not the way Heidi thinks. She understood that every life is precious, not just her own. The child in her womb was a gift from God. The Lord gives, and the Lord takes away. Ultimately, our lives belong not to ourselves, but to the God who created us and to His Son who has redeemed us. So, against all odds, and putting her faith in Christ, she forged ahead. Knowing the love of Christ and thinking about his sacrifice on the cross, how could she ever forsake that little child whom God had given her? Thanks be to God, Heidi recovered, and her child lived to see his mother's face. Heidi and Stuart named that boy Noah. How appropriate! For when we think of Noah, we are reminded that our God is a God of hope, life, and resurrection. Through all of life's storms, our Lord has promised to be with us always and to bring us, finally, from this veil of tears into life eternal. And that life is a gift to us even now.

Indeed, that is what you will find in this little treasure of a book. Little stories of life, abundant life. Heidi has surely borne her share of suffering, but in that suffering she has found joy, and it is that joy that she shares with others. And, it is not simply that Heidi has stared death in the face, but she knows what it means to live because she knows the one who alone is the Lord of Life. She well recognizes that life is not always a bowl of cherries. Since she gave birth to Noah, she's faced other challenges, including more trips to the doctors and surgeons.

This is not a book for those who want to smile and pretend that everything is okay. This is not a book for those who would like to think that the Christian life is smooth sailing. No, it's a compilation of little vignettes that help us think about our problems in a different way. It's sweet, but not syrupy. Heidi understands the human frailties and sinful shortcomings shared by us all. Her stories remind us that at times we are all too quick to judge, but then, with grace, she applies that maxim also to herself. She notices how easy it is for all of us to take for granted the little things, the small kindnesses which we Christians show to one another. And, of course, all of this is undergirded by the greater love of Christ, who suffered for our sins and who is present for us now. And this love causes us to pause and results in gratitude.

Given all this, it is not surprising that Heidi has become a popular inspirational speaker. Not of her own choosing, she is somewhat of a celebrity. Now, as we have seen in our reality-TV world, celebrity is not always such a good thing, and it can be a pointless end unto itself. But a little celebrity has its advantages. Heidi has been given the opportunity to reach out, and she takes Christ's love to places where many of us are not able to go. She has reached countless hurting women and has given them hope. Telling her story of cancer, she stands as an advocate for not only women, but for mothers and their children. Unlike other inspirational speakers, the hope she speaks of is real because it is grounded in the person of Jesus. She tells of Christ's mercy, which fills our daily lives. So, read, reflect, and enjoy. As Heidi will remind you, even in the midst of troubles, Christ's love changes everything.

Dr. Peter Scaer
Holy Week, 2011

TABLE OF CONTENTS

INTRODUCTION

These little missives are just the simple thoughts of a woman doing her best to plow through life with the best Guide imaginable. Jesus, or "JC" as I affectionately call Him, shows me endless patience, love, and compassion. He allows me to be silly or sad, confused or content, but all the while, He is taking me through the snowdrifts we all encounter in our lives.

I hope this book gives you a peek into someone else's conversations with her Lord, whether you know Him or not. He'd love to hear from you, by the way, even if you only have the alone time needed to chat while you are in the shower.

Heidi Floyd

unknown

The three of us were standing there; probably the one and only time in our lives that we would be in the same room. We were all at the same gas station at the same time.

The youngest of us was in front, paying for her gas with singles and change. I was behind you, watching you as you watched her. I saw you wrinkle your nose at her. Your eyebrows were raised as she shifted the baby from one hip to the other—that baby without shoes, just dirty little socks. You rolled your eyes when she had a hard time coming up with the last dollar owed. You barely glanced at me. I was nondescript, which in retrospect is preferable to being one deserving of your frown.

I saw her, but I saw you too. I know that your shoes and your handbag cost more than anything that the rest of us had in our closets. You live in this beautiful town; we just happened to be here to refuel on our way to or from somewhere. I have been thinking about you, and her, and me, for many days. What I wish I could tell you is that you don't know us any more than we know you.

We don't know. Perhaps, you had had a bad morning, and everything was just rubbing you the wrong way. Perhaps, you don't scowl at people less fortunate, but you had a terrible headache and your expression wasn't meant for that girl with the baby. We don't know if you had stress like we can't imagine. We just don't know. But I hope there might be an explanation like these for your reaction.

You and I don't know about that young girl. Perhaps, she made just one bad decision in her life and made a courageous choice by keeping her baby. I saw her fingers as she paid for her gas. Her bitten-down fingernails show that she might have stress like we can't imagine. The baby was dirty and barely resembled her, so the assumption that it was even her own child might be wrong. Maybe she was just helping out a friend by babysitting. We don't know whether the opportunities presented to her are a pale comparison to what we have been offered. Did she have the chance to go to college, to marry someone who might provide for her, or to work at the kind of job that would allow her to provide for herself? We don't know.

You don't know me either. I was the one you barely glanced at, a quick scan and then nothing. The young girl didn't look at either of us. She just kept her head down the whole time, so she doesn't know

anything about either of us. You don't know that
the only reason I stopped in your beautiful shop-
ping center is because I didn't want to run out of gas
before I got to the cancer center. That I knew full well
in a few hours I would be absolutely miserable and
wouldn't have the energy to stop and pump gas on
my way home.

We don't know anything about one another,
and for that, I owe both of you an apology. I was so
full of fear about my upcoming visit to the oncologist
that I didn't say "I have an extra dollar" to the girl
who so obviously needed it. I didn't pat the baby on
his cheek, which for me is standard operating procedure. I didn't smile at you when you scanned me over,
appearing to decide that I merited neither disap-
proval nor approval. Maybe that would have changed
things for a brief period of time, for the three of us.
Even if it was for just a moment, we all could have
been standing there smiling at one another instead of
retreating to our own little lonely environments.

3

I will forget my complaint,
I will put off
my sad face, and
be of good cheer.

JOB 9:27

Put on . . .
compassionate
         hearts,
kindness,
humility,
         meekness,
and patience.

COLOSSIANS 3:11–13

shoes

I like them. *Whew!* Glad I got that confession off my chest. ☺ I do keep my shoe wardrobe to a minimum, though, as I don't live in the kind of financial world that allows me to purchase dozens and dozens (as much as I'd like to do that!). Most of my shoes are the practical kind that I can wear with multiple outfits.

There is one extremely decadent pair, however, that I have in a box waaaaaay in the back of my closet. They are pink with white polka dots and have a little pink ruffle ribbon around the edge. They are peep-toe pumps with four-inch heels. Just so you know, I am a six-foot-tall woman. The combination of their decadent appearance and my height ensure that I most assuredly never wear these shoes to church. Or anywhere else out in public for that matter.

It's one of those weird little secrets that I keep and never talk about. They are wrapped up, tucked in a box, and placed in the most distant corner of my closet. Far, far away from anything other people can see.

I know people who keep God in the same kind of box and the same kind of place. He is special to them, no question. Adored. But secret. They keep God in the special spot way in the back. Out of sight from the other people in their lives.

For the most part, I think people who hide their relationship with God are doing so to be politically correct. They don't want to offend anyone. Another reason might be that it seems to be quite a popular thing to make fun of Christians, to make them appear as illiterate and primitive as possible, so they hide Him out of embarrassment. Take a look at most news Web sites today and you will see what I mean. References to Christianity usually include "objective" writers who refute or even ridicule anything that has to do with people who love God.

When people I know talk like this, I speak up when I feel they have gone too far or if I feel I can actually offer something clever to say. It seems that most of the time their standard response to me is something like, "Oh, Heidi, I don't mean *God* per se, I just mean . . . you know . . . *organized* religion." Some of these people feel they have been slighted by a church they attended in their past, and they cast the same view on anyone who likes to go to church. They want to be part of the majority who say they are Christian but they keep their faith in a box with a lid on it. Private and out of the way.

It's an odd feeling, knowing that you are a big fan of Someone who is getting a bad rap. All the critical or negative things closet Christians say are indicative of sin in this world and of sinful people, not of Jesus Himself. If they just picked up the Book, they would see what He really said, how He lived His life, and how He feels about all of us. If they joined Him on Sunday morning, they would have the courage to take the lid of their box of faith and go public with their relationship with Him. They would wear their hope in Christ with confidence.

Once they see that, there is no way they can keep Him hidden back there with the pink pumps. He would be special to them, no question. So special that they would never keep Him tucked out of the way. (P.S., I have a picture of those shoes. Lemme know if you ever want to see it. ☺)

I have not concealed
Your steadfast
love
and
Your faithfulness
from the great
congregation.

PSALM 40:9–11

peace

I am the type of person who worries. A lot. I mean all the time and about everything. Hardly the habit of a respectable Christian woman, I know. But there it is; the truth laid bare. It would be nice if I could tell you that I have never had a spirit so troubled that sleep would not come, that I have never taken a shower at 2 a.m., crying, praying, and hoping for answers. But I find myself in that spot more often than I can count.

My doctor has a familiar refrain, every time I go to see him: "You need to eliminate stress from your life, Heidi, as much as possible."

Well, really. How am I supposed to do that? There are so many things that are outside of my control; it's an impossible request! I like that I say things like that to an oncologist—he who really has life and death struggles in his hands—and I pretend like I have a lot on *my* plate. ☺

So I burn my way through every day and try to hand it all over to the Lord, without seeming too pushy. Hi, God, how are You? Um, so. Could You please help me with that missing pencil? It's just crucial; You understand. I need to find it.

I don't mean to make fun of your situation or mine, but we all think our present burdens are the most pressing of matters. Period.

Here is what my oncologist told me once, and it really did help me put things into perspective:

> Whatever your situation, stop
> for a moment and think. Are you
> rushing into surgery with an
> organ in a cooler for a transplant?
> No? Then it might not be a mat-
> ter of life and death. Therefore,
> pause, breathe, and try to relax.

So, there it is. It's hard to carry around a big load of stress all the time, so I can put those really big things—life and death—into God's hands (since that's where they are anyway). I can take a deep breath and remember that Jesus loves me, that He saves me, and that is certain. That sure is comforting.

So—next time I'm in the shower in the middle of the night, crying and praying and worrying, I will let that water washing over me remind to just trust God, to take a deep breath and relax. Because life and death matters really are outside of my control.

"Come to Me, all who labor and are heavy laden, and I will give you rest. Take My yoke upon you, and learn from Me, for I am gentle and lowly in heart, and you will find rest for your souls."

MATTHEW 11:28–29

For everything there
is a season, and a
time for every matter
under heaven:
a time to be born,
and a time to die;
a time to plant,
and a time to pluck up
what is planted;
a time to kill,
and a time to heal;
a time to break down,
and a time to build up;
a time to weep,
and a time to laugh;
a time to mourn,
and a time to dance;
a time to cast away stones,

and a time to gather
stones together;
a time to embrace,
and a time to refrain
from embracing;
a time to seek,
and a time to lose;
a time to keep,
and a time to cast away;
a time to tear,
and a time to sew;
a time to keep silence,
and a time to speak;
a time to love,
and a time to hate;
a time for war,
and a time for peace.

ECCLESIASTES 3:1–8

Roberta

My mother's name was Roberta. She lived a short life; never got to meet any of her grandchildren, didn't get to see my baby sister in her wedding dress, didn't get to know my brother's many accomplishments. There is not a day that passes that I don't think about her and miss being able to talk to her.

She was (and I say this without hesitation) the finest Christian witness I have ever known. Even when she was in the hospital days before she passed away, she spent her waking moments telling others about the love of God. She was a kind and gentle spirit, and her influence was a guiding force for my life, although our time together was too brief.

For quite some time, I have felt that void caused by her passing too soon and had what seemed like endless loneliness. When someone we love leaves us, no matter how long that person has been sick, it is almost incomprehensibly painful to our hearts. There is an emptiness that is never filled, no matter how much time passes.

Gradually, however, I began to realize that I am blessed with people who show me little glimpses of my mom. My children have her eyes, so I get to see her smiling at me every morning. I have dear friends who give me their shoulders when I need to cry it out, like she did when she was able. The same dear friends will tell me to stand up straight and behave when I need to hear it, just like my mom did.

No, I don't have my mom. And I have daily reminders of things I wish she could experience and people she would love—if only she were here.

No, I don't have my mom with me now. But here's what I do have: My sainted mom and I have a reunion in the communion of saints. Sometimes, I have a tough time understanding exactly how that happens, but I know that she's in heaven, she is praying for me, and she is restored to pain-free perfection. I know that through the blessing of God, who promises us heaven, that my mom and I will be there together one day. And through the love of our Savior, I now have so many people that I will be able to introduce to her one day.

"For this is the will
of My Father, that
everyone who looks on the Son
and believes in Him
should have eternal life,
and I will raise him up
on the last day."

JOHN 6:40

titles

We live in a world that values titles, and their perceived power, above almost everything else. The longer the title the better. The more initials after a person's name, the more impressive he or she is. I have always found it to be a delicious irony that the one Man who was of the most value for all eternity had the shortest title ever. Here is how I imagine a conversation with Jesus as He applies for the job as my own personal Savior.

me: So, thanks for stopping by. I see that you would like to be considered for the role of my Savior. And it looks like your current title is, um . . .

JC: Lord.

me: Yes, that's what it says here. Lord. That's it? I think everyone else would look for someone with a title with more . . . you know . . . syllables. I actually know a man who had to have the font reduced on his business cards just to make his title fit.

JC: Yes, I know that man. I'm the one for the job, though. You can trust Me on this. For the record, you can trust Me on everything going forward.

me: So what about Your career goals? Are you looking to climb the corporate ladder in the Heidi brand? If you start with Lord, then will you be looking to add more syllables in the future?

JC: Nope, I'm good with just that title—Lord. For you. For all eternity.

So there you have it. A simple and easy way to remember the title He has in our lives: Lord. And when we say that, we're really saying two things: First, that we know Jesus is God. Second, that we know we are His. His other titles are vast and unending; His supremacy is unequaled. The respect shown to Him should be as vast as our imaginations can provide; this is certain.

But for all His supremacy and His role as our Savior, His words are clear and easy. He is sent to us out of love, pure and simple. He is love for us. Perfect, unconditional, unchanging love. The best part of it is that He doesn't want to keep that to Himself. What He wants us to do, of course, is share it with the whole world. Give His love to everyone!

Let everyone know that He is our Savior.

He really is the only one for the job.

"A new
commandment
I give to you,
that you love one
another:
just as I have loved
you,
you also are to love
one another."

JOHN 13:33–35

a word about His love, pure and simple:

grief

Abraham and Mary Todd Lincoln's son, Willie, died when he was just twelve years old. This occurred after the couple had already lost a son at age 3. While more common then than it is now, the loss of a child was, nonetheless, completely heart wrenching for all parents. It has been said that neither of these parents completely recovered from these particular tragedies.

The loss of a child is not easily explainable, even to those with the strongest of faiths. It is my fervent wish that of all tragedies that might befall me, I might escape that one. I know that I couldn't bear it. The phrase that we might use for any other sad situation—the platitude that "everything happens for a reason"—is not appropriate. God can use everything for good, and we know that. But the death of a child is something for which our minds cannot acknowledge a purpose.

Willie Lincoln died in 1862, and the Civil War had just begun. The deadliest war in American history was full of endless tragedy. As a history buff, I realized even when I was young that these events happened in perfect sequence for God. Battles and skirmishes resulted in tens of thousands of young men dying on American fields. Abraham Lincoln saw all of those losses through the eyes of a father who had lost his own sons. He, therefore, had compassion that was unique to those who shared the experience.

Could the Gettysburg Address have been written and delivered by someone who had not been as intimate with loss? Someone who had a complete and pristine heart and not one darkened with the patina of grief? Lincoln was well known for writing personal notes of condolence to parents of fallen soldiers and for embracing these parents not only when they came to him in the White House, but also when he saw them as he stopped along roadsides as the wounded were being carried to hospitals. His own horrible loss allowed him to reach out to others in a way that no one else could have.

We have the benefit of 150 years to appreciate the intricacy of God's plan in the lives of His children who lived back then, so perhaps our view of one man's loss of his children can give context to his words that would be salve to the parents of so many others: "It is for us the living, rather, to be dedicated here to the un-finished work which they who fought here have thus far so nobly advanced. It is rather for us to be here dedicated to the great task remaining before us."

I pray that all of our tragedies be so much smaller than those mentioned here.

I also pray that the Holy Spirit gives us patience and trust that loss can help us see and do His will.

More important still, I pray that we recognize that His plan for us was accomplished through the loss of His own beloved Son. A tragedy that did have a purpose.

"So also you have sorrow now, but I will see you again, and your hearts will rejoice, and no one will take your joy from you."

JOHN 16:21–23

sleep

When we are under stress, it eludes us. When we have small children, we don't get too much of it. When those children become teenagers, we don't have it at all until they are safely home from the night's activities. As we age, we find ourselves with a myriad of new interrupters on a regular basis. It is something that we all need to survive, yet we often sacrifice it to our daily stresses and schedules.

I always look to God for my answers. Jesus slept during a storm on a boat. Big storm, little fishing boat. Slept. And soundly, too, not a restless kind of sleep. Let me emphasize what an amazing feat that is.

I've been on one cruise in my life. My father-in-law made a video of that cruise, and he would go around the table at dinner: "Here is Mom, Stuart, Alex, annnnnnnd this is where Heidi *would* be. If she wasn't getting sick. Again. Now here we have. . . ." Yes; I spent an entire cruise in a very small restroom. I'm six feet tall, so that is no small task, let me tell you. So I don't get even the physical part of that

Bible story. I couldn't accomplish that kind of deep sleep, ever, especially on a boat in a storm.

That brings us to the storms we encounter every day. The pressures of work—sometimes that alone can be the cause of lost sleep for days or even weeks at a time. Concerns for family, health, finances—all of these can plague us immeasurably and keep us awake.

Why can't we calm our minds long enough to give our bodies what we require to make tomorrow successful?

I struggle with this more than I care to think. It's not as if I don't trust that God will take care of me, I really do trust. I just wish He would send me a copy of His divine playbook so I can just flip to the end. I don't want the minute details of every play-by-play page of my life; I just want to know that the ending is a good one.

Well, the ending of *this* part of the story, that is. Because we do know, don't we, that our final ending will be happy (in the grand scheme of things). So, perhaps we can all take comfort in the unknown—why worry about what might not happen? Life is stormy. Jesus' life was really stormy. Yet, He slept on because His loving Father had everything under control. Jesus knew that the God was watching over Him, would protect Him, and would keep Him safe.

Sure the sea was rough, the shore was a long way away, and that boat was just a fragile assembly of wood. But Jesus was at peace because He knew that He was God's beloved Son.

And we are God's beloved too. It's that kind of confidence that allows us to just let go of the things we can't do anything about and rest up so we're ready to take on the things that we are given to handle. So when I consult the only divine playbook I have, I find the words I need for a good night's sleep:

In peace, I will both lie down and sleep; for You alone, O LORD, make me dwell in safety.

PSALM 4:7–8

But let all who take
refuge in You rejoice;
let them ever sing for joy,
and spread Your
protection over them,
that those who
love Your name
may exult in you.

For You bless the
righteous, O LORD;
You cover him
with favor
as with a shield.

PSALM 5:11–12

work

"It's called work for a reason, Heidi," my grandpa used to say to me. "If it were enjoyable, we'd call it 'vacation.'" He was a riot, my grandpa, and often put things in perspective for me.

As a man who was not born in this country, he was often appalled at the people who thought that a job was something one is entitled to and not something one has to seek. To him, as long as you worked hard and did your very best, your work—no matter what it was—should be respected.

The world views things through vastly different eyes than my sweet grandpa did. We are in a culture that says the lowly should be dismissed and only those who strive to climb the corporate ladder to the corner office are to be respected. Those who choose to sacrifice family time, those who forego any sort of moral structure, those who are willing to smile and deceive—the ones who would do anything to achieve a successful end result—are to be rewarded with admiration.

What a shame this is, what a sad description of our culture for all of us. There are many people who say that the American family is being ruined by a long list of anything-goes lifestyles, beliefs, and practices. A dear friend recently told me that she believes that the fall of the American family is rooted in strong part in the corporate mentality, in putting the family in second place.

I don't know about that, but it does seem to me that almost everywhere I look people are encouraged, promoted, and praised for being self-serving and ma-nipulative. And it makes one wonder what their real end result will be. Where will it stop for them? Once they achieve that level of success, will someone else be right behind them, plotting to get themselves in that position? They deceive and manipulate without recognizing that the next generation has learned all of those tricks and is now even better at the game— and to what end? I've seen too many people with big houses, big cars, big titles, and really small hearts. And I am sad for them, so sad that their lives will end one day surrounded only by the cold things that money can buy.

After He made the world, God rested. He did acknowledge that it was good, but didn't go on and on about how superfantastic He was and He didn't keep going to create something bigger and better still. He just said, "Yep, nice." And He took a break.

Everyone who works, be it in an office, a store, a car, or in a home, has this as an example. In fact, that's why God devised the days of the week the way He did—so we could take some time to rest and rejoice in Him. Yep, not bad. Perfect, even.

So why aren't we satisfied with that? Why can't we just do our best and say that it's good enough? I think it's because our culture expects perfection and we know that we're not so perfect. When we see what we do and what we are and compare ourselves to the cultural standard, we come up short.

But, really. We know where real perfection comes from; don't we? So, let's all take a day to focus only on Him and just enjoy.

On the seventh
day
God finished
His work that
He had done,
and He rested
on the seventh day
from all His work
that He had done.

GENESIS 2:1–3

Christmas

About five years ago, as you might know, I was going through a pretty tricky time in my life. Despite everything that was swirling around in my head, I was primarily concerned with Christmas. Chemo was really just beginning for me, but had already taken its toll physically, emotionally, and financially. This last thing is one that seems to last forever, and back then, I had no idea that it would be with us to this day.

As Christmas drew near, I realized that we would not be able to afford anything—*an-y-thing* for our kids. The cost of gas back and forth to treatment, the expense of taking our family along as we traveled so often to another state for that treatment, and the expenses that remained after insurance coverage stopped put us well in the red. Our credit cards were maxed out, and our finances were heading to the bleak side.

So we get home one afternoon from a trip to Indy for my treatment, and there are boxes on the front porch. Many boxes. Big boxes. Surprising boxes.

Did you order anything online? No, how could I? Did you? *No!*

Rip them open, and inside are *more* boxes, smaller and wrapped in Christmas paper. And on each box was an incredibly beautiful gift tag. I'd never seen such tags. When I turned the tags over, I saw that they had things written on the back like "Bella, age 2, wants a stuffed doggie." "Alex, age 10, wants a Millennium Falcon (Star Wars)."

That was the first arrival of boxes, but they came from that point on at least twice a week. Sometimes we received just one box, but most often there were several waiting for us at the door. Little packages, big packages, all decorated and marked with the same amazing tags indicating who the gift was for and what might be inside. (I taped them down so the kids couldn't read the contents. ☺)

That Christmas, my children knew that Mommy was pretty sick. That their little sibling was probably pretty sick too, since he was going through cancer treatment with me during that pregnancy. But they also knew that many miles away, there were some amazing people who had decided to help us by sending presents so we would still have gifts at Christmastime. Since that year, they have never received so many presents. The pile of packages was

taller than the little three-foot-tall Charlie Brown tree
we had.

The gifts were all wonderful, but for me the
best part were those tags. I didn't know until just
a few days before Christmas that my friend Kate
had made them all by hand. A mutual friend, Debbie, told me that Kate had created them herself. The
tags were hung on a tree where they worked. Anyone
who wanted to took a tag, purchased the item, and
wrapped it up. (One of the gifts was pretty hard to
find, from what I understand, and required a group
effort and a man with a big heart who was willing to
track it down.)

This most recent Christmas, like every Christmas for the past five years, I take the tags out of
a very special box and display them as part of our
home's decorations. I preserve them between panes
of glass to show my kids that when they look at the
back, they can see the hearts of the people who gave
us the presents. It looks like a simple little collage for
a festive time, but it has so much more meaning for
me. It's a reminder that people are good and kind and
generous. It's a reminder to look beyond the "thing"
so we can see the heart.

I am happy and blessed—and thankful—because all of my children, even the little guy who went through chemo with me, are healthy and safe. And now each year, we seek out other trees with tags so we can help other little ones who need a smile this Christmas.

Thank You, God, for all that we have. Love, Heidi.

Then, opening their treasures, they offered Him gifts, gold and frankincense and myrrh.

MATTHEW 2:11

indemnification

Now, how's that for a great word, huh? In-dem-ni-fi-cation. It means to compensate for damage or loss or to give security against anticipated loss. That's a big idea; to give *you security for your future*.

What are the things we might think of that can give us security, things that would compensate for that which we feel we have lost or might lose? This is so hard—we can really only wrap our minds around the material. To be secure, we probably need a million dollars . . . that way, if we lose our jobs, we can still have the house. And send the kids to college. And take trips. You know—important things like that.

For those of us who have had a rug pulled out from under us, we frequently find ourselves feeling in need of some big indemnification. Our feelings of insecurity are pervasive and fill our subconscious. Some people have lost jobs and that erodes the stability of financial peace. A relationship is tested, and we are shaky on that front as well. A home is damaged by fire or weather, and we're not sure where to turn.

What about the big stuff (and that's not to say the aforementioned aren't big, but I mean life threatening . . . or worse)? What happens when you are sitting in that chair in the examining room and the doctor says, "Yes, it's cancer. I can't believe it either; I thought for sure it was benign." Or worse (yes, there is always a "worse"), what if the pediatrician tells you that you should leave his office and begin the search for a pediatric oncologist? *Pediatric oncologist*, two words that should never ever ever ever be in the same sentence, if you ask my opinion.

What then? How do we connect with security after things like that happen? Our future is suddenly so much more finite than it was just a moment ago. Jobs, relationships, houses—those can all be mended. But a child with a broken white blood cell count?

I've always said that I don't know how people can lose a pencil or sit in traffic without faith in Jesus. When a huge challenge comes along, it is inconceivable to me that someone can make it through without Him. I rely solely on Him in all my problems. That isn't to say that I'm going to stop being a worrywart or that I will always be able to sleep soundly at night, but that's only because I have short-sighted, this-side-of-heaven human vision. It just means that I do know with certainty and for eternity, I am indemnified. Made whole. That's because Jesus has made that happen. He has already fought the good fight for me, and He promises that I don't need to fight it again. It's completely finished.

Those of us who have faith have the most amazing security for the future, and it's all been paid for up front. Now that's what I call indemnification.

> When I felt
> secure,
> I said,
> "I will never
> be shaken."
>
> PSALM 30:6 NIV

a word about my future security . . .

supervision

I asked one of my children if she understood what "supervision" meant. The reply was "well, I think it's probably something that is just way better than regular old vision." Hysterical, my children. They never cease to give me insight into how to adjust what I think I already know.

Supervision is a tricky task no matter what—or whom—you are supervising. The idea is quite simple, in theory. You are to, literally, watch over a process or a person during a task. To review the activities and give suggestions without interfering in the process or procedure is, at its core, impossible for most of us. I have never met a person who, if they see something going awry, is able to refrain from interjecting even minimal guidance (or interference). "Here, let me." "Scoot over." "No . . . just, I mean here, just, wait. . . . Oh, let me do it."

And we've all seen or been a part of the kind of hands-on interference from someone who is a micro-managing supervisor.

I have found that the supervision I have from the Lord is so different from the supervision I have from humans, and, since I am totally and thoroughly human myself, this sometimes frustrates me. How easy it would be for me if God were a micro-manager! "Scoot over, just let Me do this. You sit down and watch Me. I've got this one." It does seem to me that it would just be easier if God would make all the moves instead of letting me make mistakes as I try to make the moves.

However, the more I give over to Him, the more I find that that really is the way God supervises. He does watch over me with super vision because He sees all things. He does guide, with a strong yet compassionate hand. He has endless patience with me as I repeatedly fail at my tasks. And He still allows me to learn from those failures.

His methods of supervision are far more guidance-oriented than anything humans can offer. It's ironic, isn't it? that the one Guy who has all the answers allows us to try to figure things out ourselves. Go figure.

And the truth is that God really does "have" this one. I mean, He's the one with the master plan, and He's the only one who can make it happen. Because we can't fix the problem of the brokenness in this world, the problem caused by sin, God scooted us aside and fixed it—through Jesus. When we look at it that way, we see that God is as hands-on a supervisor as possible. He has the end result already worked out. He has the procedure already in place. He sent His own Son to be right here in our midst, in the flesh, one of us, to love us and do the work of salvation for us.

"Here," God says. "Just let Me do this."

I'm so thankful He's done that. I'm thankful that He's our Supervisor.

Lead me in Your truth and teach me, for You are the God of my salvation; for You I wait all the day long.

PSALM 25:4–6

rerun

Some years ago, there was a television show called *M*A*S*H*. For a while, it seemed as if reruns of it were on every hour of the day. It was finite, of course, so the reruns were repeated. I have a friend whose college claim to fame was that he had seen every single *M*A*S*H* episode. This was quite a feat in the days before DVDs and DVR and instant internet access to everything! Of all of the television programs I've ever seen, I think there are perhaps two or three that I would consider watching more than once.

The limits of human imagination are so evident in the way our world finds its entertainment. It's sad, to me, that so much of what our culture considers to be entertainment is in the form of cruelty disguised as competition or fun in the guise of humiliation. (Very disheartening!) That kind of entertainment is not something I want to see again. It's old and stale.

But there is one place that I find reruns to be always new, always fresh, always something beneficial—the Bible. Each story is new every time, because I am a new person every time I read it. For example, when I first read the story of Dinah, I was a young person who found the entire story, beginning to end, repulsive. Honestly, it took me several times to read through it in its entirety. There are many different interpretations of her story, but the one I am comfortable with is the one that includes Dinah *not* being assaulted. It was a misinterpretation of the facts, something like that. He loved her, that Shechem. And the history of Dinah's brothers lead me to suspect that they have a bit of a shady side. Just tossing the idea out there.

To me, seeing something new every time I read it is the best part of the Bible. I have Bibles of every size and shape, even one in pink. I have an online edition and a hundred-year-old German edition. Every form, every version is mine to explore over and over again and to savor each time. God's Word for me has been my solace in my darkest hours, my calming source in troubled times, and my words of compassion when I couldn't find any in my own mind.

The best reruns are found there. I encourage you to take a closer look at your favorite parts. And your least favorite, as well. You might find a new way to look at something you didn't like before. You might find some new message.

Or not. After all, God is always the same.

Reading
from the scroll
the words
of the LORD
in the LORD's house.

JEREMIAH 36:7–9

forgiveness

I have a very dear friend who was treated quite poorly just before she left her job. It was so distressing to talk to her and learn about what was occurring to her every day; she is such a kind, sweet person! I could not understand why these things would happen to someone so wonderful.

After she left that job (against her will!), I had lunch with her. It had been just a few weeks, and she looked wonderful. The stress that had been etched in her face was far less visible than it was before. She was quite at peace with the way things were going in her life now, and it was beautiful to see.

Here's the best part, however: She had forgiven all the nastiness that had been done to her. Completely. She hadn't forgotten, but as we talked about it, it was clear that it just *didn't matter anymore*. She had closed that door in her life and was totally at peace with the fact that she was in a different spot and God was blessing her there. She had even corresponded with the person who had caused her so much grief!

I don't know about you, but I have a terrible habit of being unable to let go of injustices done to myself or to those whom I love. The words "I forgive you" so easily roll off my tongue, but real forgiveness—like my friend gives—eludes me sometimes. Once a trust is violated, it's just so difficult to look the offender in the eyes, isn't it?

Yet, I realize every time I don't forgive someone, I continue to let their past hover like a dark cloud. I myself am violating a trust. God has forgiven me for all the things I have done, for all the things I try not to do but repeat nonetheless. That was His whole point in sending Jesus to live and die for me.

I'm forgiven. Every day. The cross is proof. That's where I look to be reminded of that forgiveness. And no matter how much I want to hold on to past injustices, I know that forgiving them is beautiful. And if I ever forget, He has given me my sweet friend as a great example right here on earth.

Bearing with
one another
and, if one
has a complaint
against another,
forgiving each
other;
as the Lord
has forgiven you,
so you also must
forgive.

COLOSSIANS 3:12–14

in-laws

When I was almost nine, my parents brought home an extraordinary package. She was little, pink, and cried quite a bit. She was also someone who was bound immediately to my very heart and soul, just as my older brother was. As she grew up, she touched all of my things when I didn't want her to, she came in my room repeatedly when I had given express orders to the contrary, and she had the audacity to be cute. Much cuter than me; brutally unfair.

As someone said in an Indiana Jones movie, she left "just when she was getting interesting." We all did. Just when I found my brother to be not only tolerable but actually worth talking to—BAM!—off he goes to the Navy. I did pass the time in amusing fashion by calling whatever base he found himself stationed, phoning the CO, asking for "Billy." (Okay, that only happened once, but it was delightful.) Then, he got married, had a little boy . . . and grew a life all his own.

When she was older, my sister brought home a package of her own. He came in the form of a first-generation German man with a dry wit and a great sense of humor. *Who does he think he is,* I wondered. *Heather is just a baby!* No possible way this guy is going to be someone I like. Ever. Of course, it took about 5.2 seconds for me to realize that I might just indeed like him, and he was probably perfect for her.

Our families come in so many formats, such varied groupings. And just when you think you have a grasp of the structure, it is bound to change. We are by nature resistant to change, especially change in our families whom we hold so dear. Inclusion of new entities are often as resisted as the departure of original members, yet both have a purpose to God.

What a blessing a family can be, no matter how small or large. The changes that we experience in our families are all part of His plan for us, although we may not see it at the time. I pray that you, too, can enjoy and welcome all changes that come to your family. Even if they come in the form of a dry and witty German or a new bundle of someone cuter than you.

Trust in the LORD with all
your heart, and do not lean on
your own understanding.

PROVERBS 3:5

a word about my family blessings:

talent

I have four children, each of them with remarkably unique talents. And no matter how I think their talents should be harnessed, every day I am taught that that is completely out of my hands. I can suggest, cajole, prompt, and even beg; but if it isn't in God's master plan for them, then none of my effort will matter.

My little ones all have wonderful singing voices. Beautiful, in fact. My eldest is always ready to break into song and is willing to share that talent on stage or in the choir loft; wherever is needed. My second daughter, however, is completely reluctant to sing when anyone else can see or hear her.

One evening as she was singing in her shower, I asked her if she would like to sing in church. "Oh, *no*, Mommy, I would never do that! People would look at me, and I just *can't!*" she exclaimed in abject horror. *Why, God,* I thought, *would You give such a talent to someone who has to keep it under wraps? That doesn't* make sense to me. Perhaps, I should just force her. *I am the mommy, after all,* I thought, as the infinite power of mommy-ness swept across me.

As I was in the shower myself, and talking it over with Jesus (the only place I have alone time, busy working mom and all), it seemed to me that He asked why I was so pushy about this. Didn't I trust that He had a plan for my daughter? Display and use of this and, actually, any talent my children have were not for me to decide. Totally His call.

Ridiculous, I said (I only say things like that in my head. It's never a good idea to get into vocal disputes with the Risen Savior). I was out of the shower and on to other things, but I was still muttering something about "wasted talent; I think I *know* what is good for my babies," when I heard it. Catie was singing, and not in the shower.

It was a quiet, gentle song. She was in the basement, way back in the corner, so I had to walk all the way around to see what she was doing. Her little brother had fallen on a toy, and I hadn't heard him. He was crying and scared, and she had come to his rescue. She was singing him a lullaby and holding him in the most tender way.

I asked if everything was okay, and Noah said, "Yes, Mommy. I got hurted and Catie is making me all better." I told them both how splendid I thought that was. "She always does, Mommy. When I am scared, Catie sings me a song. Always."

And there it was. That non-wasted talent. That amazing and perfect use of a blessed gift. It was not something I knew about or something I had orchestrated, and yet I was able to witness the plan. What a wonder it would be if we could all get a glimpse of things we never expect to see coming and enjoy them in such a sweet way.

Oh sing to the LORD
a new song;

sing to the LORD,
all the earth!

PSALM 96:1–3

Sing praises
    to the LORD,
O you His saints,
 and give thanks
to His holy name.

 For His anger
is but for a
moment,
   and His favor is
    for a lifetime.

Weeping may tarry
   for the night,
 but joy comes
with the morning.

PSALM 30:4–5

joy

We all have big moments we can immediately recall to share when anyone asks about things that made us happy. Wedding days, births of children, a major success in work or play—really grand events are the easiest way to express the joys we've felt.

The everyday is a much more difficult statement for joy, though, isn't it? We have routine, pressure, tasks, the mundane and monotonous that fill our every waking moment. A moment of joy has to shine fairly brightly to be noticed in the day-to-day operations of normalcy.

I made a promise to myself a few years ago that I would find those joys on a daily basis. This has not been without its challenges, let me assure you. There are times when I just push through the day and feel like a wet washcloth by the time I get to bed; why would I have made myself that promise? Finding joy every day? Impossible.

It was a gift; a promise to oneself is always a gift. I made that promise after I had completed my chemo treatments, so I was pretty familiar with difficult circumstances. But I was resolved to do it anyway, no matter what occurred.

We are surrounded by people who are restlessly unhappy. It is an amazing thing to be around others whose life journeys seem to be far less complicated. There are actually television programs focused on people who just have a *dire need* for houses that cost millions of dollars on the coast of some exotic locale. I could let the children watch and yearn for such things, but that shows them a path of little joy. Instead, I teach them that we have a remote control—turn it off and let's make some cookies instead! Instant joy!

On the dropping-like-a-washcloth-at-the-end-of-the-day days that I so frequently have, I drag myself home and feel like I have nothing to offer in my daily joy report. Sometimes, those days involve my coming home well after the entire household has gone to bed. (Yes, I know that having a job and a home are joys in and of themselves. I'm trying to be poignant.) And it is then that I go and give good-night kisses to the best joys I have ever known.

Thank You, God!

The LORD
your God
will bless you
in all your
produce and
in all the work
of your hands,
so that you
will be altogether
joyful.

DEUTERONOMY 16:14–16

fishies

"Excuse me," she said. "Is that your car?"

Oh, no . . . what did I do? Park in the wrong spot? Run over something? (Have you noticed I have a tendency to panic and assume the worst?)

her: "Well, the reason I ask is that, um, well I saw your fish."

me: Blink. Blink. Blink. "Fish?"

her: "The little fish. On the back by your license plate. Are you a Christian?"

Ohhhhhhhh! My *fish!* Gotcha.

It turns out that she was new to the area and hadn't found many people to connect with. When you find yourself in a new place and looking for someone with similar interests, it's hard to tell much about them just by looking. We connect by little signals we send each other. (You would be surprised how many complete strangers will come up to you in an airport and talk to you if you have a pink ribbon on your lapel, for example.)

So, I bought that fish ten years prior, at the same time I bought the car. I had saved up enough to put down a substantial down payment and was so proud to get it. The last thing I wanted on it was something like a bumper sticker or anything like that. (Of course, in a few years, my husband would decide it needed a CTS bumper sticker—but that is a story for another book.)

The fish was perfect, I thought. *It was subtle, but it said all I needed to say.* The only other ornamentation was the service flag I have in my window for my brother and brother-in-law. (I'm crazy proud of our military.) So I put the fish on my car and forgot about it. For ten years. Until my new friend saw it.

Now, I have a new opportunity to visit with someone who reached out to me specifically because she saw that ancient symbol for Christianity on my car and understood that it means that I am a believer in Christ. She wants to talk to someone who she can share her thoughts, prayers, and concerns with and not worry about being judged. She wants to have lunch with someone who folds her hands before digging in.

I need a new car now. My old one has been driven into the ground, that poor car. But I can tell you that although a few months ago I wouldn't have given a second thought to getting another fishie, now I think I will get one of those before I even look for a new car.

"Follow Me,
and I will make
you become
fishers of men."

MARK 1:16–18

a word about little signals of God in my heart . . .

Croatoan

In 1587, a group of English settlers formed a colony off the coast of what is now North Carolina. Three years after it was settled, another group of travelers came to the Roanoke Island colony. There was no trace of anyone from the first colony; all the English settlers had completely disappeared. There were no signs of distress or trouble; it was as if they had just vanished into thin air. The one and only clue left was the word CROATOAN carved into a tree or post. To date, there are many theories about what had occurred, but there are no definitive answers. No remains of colonists were ever located.

This is a fabulous mystery that has filled me with intrigue since I was a little girl. When I was young, Croatoan, the Oak Island lost treasure, and Amelia Earhart would occupy hours of my time in the local public library. I read everything anyone had written on those subjects; I was mesmerized by the drama and romance of it all. What had happened, who did what and when? And most important, were UFOs involved? (When I was a child, it seemed like every mystery could be solved by either calling in Nancy Drew or saying it was a UFO.)

I would love to someday learn the answers to those questions. I just want to know.

Everyone I know has a little list of things they, too, want to know. "When I get to heaven, I'm going to ask God about this" is something I hear a lot. Some of these mysteries are quite complex, like why someone they loved died young or why things like natural catastrophes occur, etc.

After rereading Revelation for the hundredth time, I have finally come to the realization that I might not get the chance to ask any questions. The description of heaven is enough for me to realize that I will be so entranced by eternal majesty and so filled with joy and peace as I worship with "all the company of heaven" that nothing else will matter.

In the here and now, though, I still want to know about the mysteries surrounding us on earth, as do most people I know. But I am also anxious to meet the me who doesn't care anymore; the me I will be in the most "people place" ever created.

Having the glory
of God,
its radiance
like a most
rare jewel,
like a jasper,
clear as crystal.

REVELATION 21:11

worse

I was eight months pregnant with my son. Six days earlier, I had a chemo treatment that left me kind of tired. I'd already lost all of my hair and was just feeling low. Things don't get much worse, right? Wrong.

That day, my sweet little Isabella, then two years old, was feeling bad so I took her to the doctor. She said she had a headache, and we knew that was unusual for a small child, so I took her in.

Our regular pediatrician, a wonderful, strong woman, was out of the office for a few days, so we were shown to her new partner. He was young and new to the profession, but trying hard to make sure everything was just exactly the way it was supposed to be.

He looked at me, looked at her. He asked me what my story was; I gave him the CliffsNotes-fifty-cent version. I'm pregnant and I have cancer. I was seated, with Bella on my lap. There are a few things that have happened in my life that, when I recall them, I will always remember all the details, exactly where I was, whether I was sitting or standing, and where the other person was as well. This is one of these moments. Bella was quiet and sweet, snuggled on my lap. Her hair was soft and blond and up in a little ponytail. The doctor was sitting across from me, and he reached over to touch my knee. He said, "I think what we need to do is find a pediatric oncologist."

Right there, I realized how much worse things could be.

In all honesty, if I wasn't pregnant, I would have never gone through the chemo. The only thing that made me want to stick with it and fight was that child, that little unborn baby that I was told to terminate. By now, I knew the full scope of what it was like being a cancer patient. I didn't qualify for surgery-and-you-are-done, like so many of my dear cancer friends. I had to go the distance—chemo, surgeries, and radiation, followed by years of more junk. I knew my horizon and my heart was shattered to think that my darling Bella could face the same.

The following day, our regular pediatrician came back, and she called me to bring Bella in; she just wanted to have a look-see of her own before we went down that path. When I got there, she looked at the file and chatted for awhile. "Did they do a blood draw on Bella yesterday? I can't find any results here."

"No," I told her, "they tried but her little veins blew so they couldn't." She got the most incredible look on her face: part anger, part frustration, part wonder. She stormed out of the examining room, but I could hear her say, "Get this child's blood *right this minute!*"

And they did.

What she explained to me later, after she looked at the test results, was that my little Bella-Boo had anemia, just like me, not cancer (just like me). The iron in her blood was so low that her heart was in jeopardy, so we had to immediately take her to the hospital next door. Bella was strapped down to me so they could give her a complete blood and platelet transfusion. They tied us together, head to toe, with the exception of her small right foot, which was taped to a wooden block. They made an incision to find a vein, a procedure I'd never even seen on TV. It was horrifying.

She and I were all alone after they started the transfusion, and I watched her color change from gray to pink, starting right there at her foot and working its way up to her smile. It was so scary for me, but I just clung to her as tightly as she was clinging to me. I prayed that if there was a choice to be made, that I be the one to suffer and not her. Please, please God.

She stayed in the hospital for a while where the staff could watch her, but we were assured that she would be okay. We had to stop giving her whole milk, as that was like poison to her system. Although she didn't like meat, we had to force her to eat it, and spinach, etc. Iron drops stained her teeth gray, but we didn't care.

Bella now rarely has a day that she isn't covered with chocolate and a smile. She has recovered perfectly. But we never have whole milk in our house. I never serve iceberg lettuce; doctors told me it's worthless and won't help anyone. We eat spinach instead; it's a small price to pay, considering.

I doubt there are many people that know this story because there were so many other things going on with our family. I tell you this now to say that, yes, I know you are having a bad day, bad week, bad month. I know you feel slighted and hurt, rejected and betrayed. You have hatred in your heart for someone who might feel the same way you do or who might not even care. You have focused all of your energy on making sure that things go well for you. But there are other things that are so much more important! Yes, your life is hard. Believe me when I tell you, that I totally understand that. There are things worse even than cancer, and if you've got the time, we can commiserate about that list of things.

But just know that worse is out there. Worse things, worse people, worse situations. Look in the eyes of a parent who has lost a child and you realize that your little woes are not even worth discussion. As you sit in your favorite chair and click onto your Facebook page to see/stalk/criticize/comment/share/discuss, just realize that by nature of the fact that you are in a warm cozy house with a computer and internet connection, you are better off than seventy percent of the world, if not more. How are your children? Well, one son is married to a horrible girl, I *hate* her. My child is not working the job he should have, I just know it. My daughter has just made such bad choices, and I don't know what to do to help her. My two-year-old is constantly throwing temper tantrums; I can't take it any more! My youngest just climbed up on my kitchen counter—what is the deal with that? My husband has to take all that medicine and it's ruining my life. That teenager is a write-off in my mind; not even worth saving or discussing anymore.

Here's the point; if you still have them in your lives to complain about, you should be thankful. No one is a write-off, and hating is not only wrong, it's a waste of time. Today, I am thankful for my Bella and for what a gift she is to me in my life. And to Alex and Catie and Noah. They are all gifts to me and to one another. The people in my family—

in-laws, step-relations, out-laws—all of them are gifts to me. I can learn from them and benefit from everyone. And God put them in my life just like He put me in theirs. For this, I am thankful.

> Thank You, Lord, for all of those
> selfless people who do apheresis
> donations, for the doctors who are
> old and wise and know without
> panic what is the matter. But mostly,
> for allowing that little foot to finally
> accept the needle and make my
> precious baby all better. Amen.

And implored Him earnestly,
saying,
"My little daughter
is at the point of death.
Come and lay Your
hands on her,
so that she may be made
well and live."

MARK 5:22–24

mixer

I've always wanted a KitchenAid mixer. They look so sleek and professional. And since I bake and cook quite a bit, it would definitely be a well-used appliance. But the cost has always been prohibitive, so one has never found its way to my counter. There are a handful of people who have asked me what I would like for Christmas, and to them the cost of a KitchenAid would be—shall we say, pocket change—so I've thought about telling them.

God has a plan for each and every one of us, even if we are far too daft to realize it sometimes. We have what we have *and* what we lack for a reason. For a purpose. For an answer to a question we don't even know we are asking. I see this every day, and so do you. Sometimes, we just forget to open our eyes and look around to see the great answers God gives us.

The answer He has given me about the Kitchen-Aid mixer is no. A resounding *no*. Not a wishy-washy parental "welllllll, maybe if you quit whining," but a big fat no. Pooh pooh pooh, poor me. Why not? I will use it *all* the time *and* I finally have a counter big enough for one. "Because," He tells me. "Open your eyes. The reason why you don't need a mixer—why you *can't* have a mixer—is right in front of you."

And indeed, this morning, there was my answer. My sweet little daughter came up to me, as she does every Saturday, and said, "Pancake Day, Mommy!" Her siblings gathered to get the ingredients, one the flour, one the baking powder, one the milk, etc. Then, very slowly, very carefully, they started to whisk. By hand. We do this ritual every Saturday. We talk, we laugh, we sing. They learned to measure and to spell *milk*, *oil*, *flour*, etc., at a very early age because we went over it once a week on Pancake Day. They learned to take turns and to be careful and slow. They learned how much fun it is to sift flour. They learned that spilling pancake batter shouldn't make you cry and that cloth is better than paper towels to clean up said batter.

This is why I don't have a KitchenAid mixer. And why I won't ask for one now. I think I'll wait until my little son goes to college. Or medical school.

For the record, Lord, I don't see why Le Creuset cookware isn't an option. We could all use it together. . . .

Many are the plans
in the mind
of a man,
but it is the purpose
of the LORD
that will stand.

PROVERBS 19:20–22

can't

"Take a look at this, Heidi, and figure it out. I want you to learn what they did and re-create it for me," said the Big Boss Man. And I mean that literally, in every sense of the word. He was three hundred pounds of Chicago by way of Sicily and he owned the company. "I can't," I told him. "I'm not the one you want," I said. I'm an underwriter at an insurance company, for crying out loud. I don't do *computer* stuff."

"But," he said, "you are the one that fixes the copier and the printers and stuff. It's all computers."

"That makes no sense," I said. "None whatso-ever. There is *no way* I can do what you are asking me. No way." But he doesn't stop looking at me and smiling. "Sure you can. Just do it."

So I take this thing home, this new project. In my head, I am still saying this is not something I should even have in my hands. It is well beyond what I can do. Why on earth would he have put this on me? There are professionals out there to do this kind of thing!

It dawns on me, about two minutes after I open it on my computer, that I like this stuff. I really, really like it. More important, I understand it. It's a bit more complex than anything I'd seen so far, but it all made sense to me. The project was a large one, so it took me about a week. By the end of that week, however, I had finished what the Big Boss Man had asked of me. And I had even customized it to include a few tweaks that I knew he would like. Another week, he had reports structured around that data.

Two months later, every department in the company had their own customized versions. I had found a new career, a new passion, a new skill set. All because someone told me I could do something when I was confident that I could not. And he was so matter-of-fact about it. I learned so much from the Big Boss Man, including how to properly smoke a good cigar. Someone having confidence in us is often all we need to be pushed in the right direction.

There are so many remarkable aspects to this story. First, that someone of his importance would believe in and give such an opportunity to an employee with no experience is amazing. That he encouraged me when I was clearly resistant to the idea—and even told him no on several occasions—also staggering.

It was a pivotal point in my life, and I didn't even realize it at the time. Looking back, I can see it as the beginning of a new chapter of my life. I am grateful and have given prayers of thanksgiving for that Big Boss Man since then. We have long since fallen out of touch with each other, but I am hopeful that someday I might see him again. We can go out for cigars, and I can tell him that he was a blessing from God.

I can't wait to see the look on his face when I tell him that.

I could strengthen you
with my mouth,
and the solace of my lips
would assuage your pain.

JOB 16:4–6

prayer

The prayers were constant, day after day for almost a full year. Variations on the same theme, but all desperate attempts to change a fairly bad situation. Nothing was improving. As a point of fact, things were getting much worse.

I am talking to You, Lord, but nothing is happening. Nothing good, I mean.

I meet a woman for breakfast; we haven't met in person until now, but we have chatted online before. I know she is a Christian because that was the subject of our discussions. I'm on a business trip in her city, and she has exactly one hour before her daughter's softball game. As soon as we meet, she says, "I've got this Bible study book for you. I believe that I am supposed to pass this to you, and to tell you that you are praying wrong.'"

Praying wrong? Incorrect praying? Is that even possible? I thought any time you chatted with Jesus, you were good to go.

She explained that my situation, although she had just the smallest amount of information about it, indicated that I was praying for the wrong thing. "His will," she said. "Focus on that."

But I thought I had been! I always include the "if it is Your will" phrase! (Okay, it was usually wrapped in a laundry list of what I thought would be best, but God knows that's how I work. He's crazy patient with me.) I mean, this was a really important thing that I wanted, and it was dissolving before my eyes. Why isn't He just fixing it already?

She said that I need to pray from an entirely different mind-set. Pray for that person, period. Pray that God will make them to be what *He* wants, to mold that person to be what *He* needs them to become. Then, she said, "Pray that *you* can help that person to fulfill what God needs. Stop worrying about what you think it should be, what you think anyone needs to become. Let God create this path, and then *follow it*. No matter how hard, just trust that He is laying the stones for you to walk."

So I did what she said, and I changed how I prayed. Still with ferocity, with fervor, with an open heart begging for help. But I prayed that we would become what He wanted. At this moment in time, I don't know that the problems are gone entirely, but I can tell you, with some degree of certainty, that I am changing the manner in which I pray.

That in and of itself is an accomplishment!

I've shared that little book with so many friends; it's just a beautiful, simple piece of work. I'm thankful for all of it, and for my online friend who took time away from her busy schedule to deliver a new way to look at the Word of God.

Continue steadfastly in prayer, being watchful in it with thanksgiving.

COLOSSIANS 4:1–3

Jesus

I have friends who are not Christians. Many of them have identical traits and sentiments, and I find that fascinating. They are all kind and compassionate, generous, and willing to go the extra mile for their fellow human beings. The sentence I seem to always hear from them is: "Oh, I don't hate God. I just don't like organized religion."

Organized and *religion*—I smile to myself every time I hear those words together. If they only knew, right? The only reason most churches are even remotely organized is because there are groups of ladies in the congregations who have more self-discipline and organizational skills than the marine corps!

But I know what these friends of mine are referring to. I really do. At some point, someone made sure to tell them that God doesn't like them. And that's terrible.

Everyone who reaches adulthood understands that there are consequences to their actions. We all know that there will be punishment for wrongdoing, and that punishment comes in various forms. We are shown that on a daily, sometimes hourly, basis.

What we aren't given as adults is compassion. That's why when people do amazingly kind deeds, it makes the news. These adults, my friends who are not Christians, were never told about the compassionate Jesus. They only got the you-are-in-so-much-trouble Jesus. No wonder they feel so unwanted in church! They have decided that if He hates them so much, perhaps He doesn't want to be a part of their lives.

There isn't a week that goes by that I don't tell someone about Jesus. And that He loves them, and loves them a whole lot more than they've been told. A whole lot more than anyone else ever will or can. Yes, of course He wants them to behave, but don't we all? Most of all, Jesus wants us to be saved because He *loves* us. ☺

You know someone like these friends of mine; I know you do. Someone who feels that "church" is "bad." They are telling you that they have been hurt, and terribly. You know that someone out there representing our wonderful Jesus either communicated poorly or maybe misunderstood Him themselves and decided to spread the word that He only wants the perfect people to make it to heaven. That's not true. As a matter of fact, it's absolutely false. I have this

Book that says otherwise. Here's a sample of what this Book says: "Those who are well have no need of a physician, but those who are sick. I came not to call the righteous, but sinners" (Mark 2:17).

Plus, if Jesus only wanted flawless people up there with Him, this Book I have wouldn't say things like this: "The Son of Man came to seek and to save the lost" (Luke 19:10). Or this one: "For God so loved the world, that He gave His only Son, that whoever believes in Him should not perish but have eternal life" (John 3:16). And the verse that comes after that: "For God did not send His Son into the world to condemn the world, but in order that the world might be saved through Him" (John 3:17).

Did you catch that? God sent Jesus to the world. The whole world. Not to condemn us but to save us. And just so you know, I'm going to do all I can to share that news with as many people as I can—even the naughty ones.

Take My yoke
upon you, and
learn from Me,
for I am gentle
and lowly
in heart,
and you will find
rest for your souls.

MATTHEW 11:28–30

Blessed are the poor in spirit,
    for theirs is the kingdom
of heaven.

Blessed are those who mourn,
    for they shall be comforted.

Blessed are the meek,
    for they shall inherit
                    the earth.

Blessed are those who hunger
and thirst for righteousness,
    for they shall be satisfied.

Blessed are the merciful,
    for they shall receive mercy.

Blessed are the pure in heart,
    for they shall see God.

Blessed are the peacemakers,
for they shall be called
sons of God.

Blessed are those who
are persecuted for righteousness'
sake, for theirs is the kingdom
of heaven.

Blessed are you when others
revile you and persecute you and
utter all kinds of evil against
you falsely on my account.

Rejoice and be glad, for
your reward is great in heaven,
for so they persecuted the
prophets who were before you.

MATTHEW 5:3–12

empty

There are several ladies in my life that have empty homes right now. Well, not totally *empty*. What I mean is that they live alone. Some are quite young, finished college recently, and are just starting out. Some of them have college just a bit farther back in the rearview mirror, if you know what I mean. ☺ It's funny how they both view their homes, their lives, their futures.

The youngest say things like "I can't *wait* to get this place by myself. It will be so wonderful to be able to do what I want, when I want and *no one* will be around to get in my way or tell me I can't or I have to or take the remote control. This will be amazing!" Then, about two weeks into their big, fabulous alone time, they start calling friends. "Wanna come over, see my place? No, no, don't leave yet! Stay for awhile! Want some tea? Anything?" They have learned that alone time means really alone, empty. For them, by yourself for hours on end isn't the sweet deal they imagined it would be. Yes, of course, it is a gift, most of the time. But then there are moments when they wish it wasn't quite so empty.

Some of my older friends are alone by something other than their choice. They have lost spouses, and the kids and grandkids live hours and hours away. I often find that they immediately start conversations from the opposite end of the spectrum. "How on earth am I supposed to stay in that empty house all by myself? There is no redeeming value to that much alone time." But then, gradually, they realize that living alone need not be the end of their world as much as they thought it would be. One lady told me, "I put stuff away, I do the dishes, and it stays that way! I've never had that happen before! I can now be as much of a neat freak as I want!" Of course, this was a gradual appreciation; it does take time to find the blessings in everything.

My sweet grandma is someone whose example I will follow as much as I am able. After years of taking care of my grandpa with Alzheimer's (and this was back when nursing homes would not accept him, the disease was just too "new" and not fully understood), she was faced with living in an empty home. Well, partially. My grandpa passed away at the end of my senior year of high school, and after he died, I spent the summer with her. I'd like to state for the record that a group of women in their seventies made this teenager exhausted. I couldn't keep up with their sass and energy.

Anyway, when I left at the end of that first summer, I asked her if she was afraid of being alone. She told me that she had an elaborate network of friends who would watch out for her; so, no, she wasn't concerned. She also wanted to travel, and she and one of her friends had already booked their first trip. The house she had shared with Grandpa was hard for her to be in, but she decided that she just wasn't going to let it best her. She would use the house as a way station, simply a place to sleep and prepare for the next adventure that would come along. She volunteered at the library and at church. She found every buffet in the tri-state area that offered senior discounts to those who ate dinner at 4 p.m. Stuff like that. But she never allowed the "empty" to overtake her heart. Her prayers were strong and steadfast and helped her every minute.

I don't know if I will be the last one in our empty house one day. Health dictates that I very well might not be, but I can promise you this—I will never really be alone. And neither will you, because there is One who is our constant companion, comforter, encourager, and friend. He reassures us of that fact when He promises that He "will never leave you nor forsake you" (Hebrews 13:5). No doubt about it!

But, if some day I am in an empty house and you decide to come for a visit, please call first. I fully intend to follow in the footsteps of my grandma as much as I can . . . and those buffets better offer plenty of dessert!

Will You never look away from me, or let me alone even for an instant?

JOB 7:18–20 NIV

checkbox

We've all been asked to fill out survey forms, either online or on paper, that compile information about us that the surveyor thinks is important. Check a box, these forms request, to identify us by relationship, nationality, age, or religion, for example. Check a box to indicate what we think about something or how we feel about an experience.

Paper versions of surveys are so much easier, aren't they? When the creators of these forms indicate that we can "select all that apply," we use our pencils and scribble in as many of those little boxes as we feel are appropriate to us. (As a child, I would check both "German" and "American" whenever those options were given. You'll not meet a bigger fan of my beloved homeland, but I can still hear my grandpa's voice in his lovely German accent; that was my silent and heretofore unannounced homage to him.)

But online versions of survey forms are totally different. If researchers are looking for a specific answer from us, we can't check more than one box. Our first choice is unchecked if we decide to go to another.

What happens is that our race, age, marital status, choice of church, and family status now become reduced to a little spot in a little square. The freedom wielded by a number 2 pencil is rendered completely obsolete and we have to become comfortable with just one choice. Betcha never thought you would miss a simple pencil until you find yourself yelling at a document saying "but I'm both German and American!" or "what do you mean, 'family' or 'friend' . . . my family are my friends!" These online forms don't allow us the flexibility of identifying ourselves in more than one way.

I think that if God had a survey form, it would be a pretty simple one and it wouldn't allow flexibility either. I think He would just ask: "Do you love Me? Check yes or no." There is no option for an essay, no "maybe" or "sometimes" or rate an answer on a sliding scale. There is no "yes . . . if or when." No room for us to say something conditional like "Well, sure I love You and everything, God. But I have a few questions before I go any farther. Jericho, Delilah, Enoch, Mark . . . if You would just give me the whole story, then I'd be happy to check the box." There's no accommodation for our argumentative nature either: "Well, Lord, sometimes I get really angry about the stuff that's happening on this planet, so I'm not sure if I like You today. Yes, I know that we humans caused some of this ruckus ourselves, but I am feeling petulant and I don't feel like owning up to how our sin has destroyed things, so I don't really know what I want to say on this form of Yours."

The truth is that we won't understand all of God's plan while we're here on earth. And there are going to be plenty of moments that drag into days, months, years, and decades, even, when we feel that things aren't going our way. But however we respond to Him with how we feel in the moment, we are still loved. During extended times when we have so much need and so many wants that appear to go unresolved, we are still loved. Even when something happens that is so horrific that we feel hurt and angry and unlovable, we are still loved. Even when we hear news about disasters that just don't make sense, we are still loved.

Maybe the question God's form really asks is, "Do you know how much I love you? Check yes or no."

She said, "Yes, Lord."

MATTHEW 15:27

close

A few years ago, we were incredibly blessed by being able to take our children on a vacation to Disney World. I love Disney World, and I would be overjoyed at the prospect of taking my children back there again. But the best part wasn't the location; it was that we were all there together.

We stayed in the Animal Kingdom Resort. The reason that hotel was chosen was simple; after our last child was born, we exceed the number of people allowed in a standard hotel room. We can't afford the luxury of big family vacations, typically, so until this trip, we didn't know that we had grown to the point of needing two hotel rooms. That arrangement would double our vacation costs. Yikes!

Well, our room in this wonderful hotel seemed perfect, at least to me. There were bunk beds, a Murphy bed, a crib, and a king-size bed for Mommy and Daddy. Amazing! There we all were, snug and cozy in one room, with a balcony view of giraffes to boot. It was absolute paradise. (I don't think I've ever seen my children so happy to wake up and run to the window—

and that includes snow days and Christmas.) The space might have seemed tight to many people, but I can't recall sleeping better anywhere else than I did in that room.

This was just two months after completing my radiation therapy for cancer, so sleep wasn't a close acquaintance of mine. A feeling of dread had been hovering over me for oh, so long, and it revolved around my family. My worries about their well-being permeated my every thought, and it was my most challenging struggle. It wasn't a surprise for me to learn that a frequent habit of cancer patients is to wake in the middle of the night and check on their family members while they sleep. Sometimes, this habit stays with the patients for the rest of their lives, causing them to forfeit a good, solid night's sleep from that point on. I tell you without hesitation that I fall into that category.

But on this vacation, I slept. Well. Once that door was closed, and all four of my children—safe and warm and tired—were within five feet of me in that room, I felt secure. More so than I'd felt in quite some time.

When people talk about heaven, I think of that place and time. The debates can rage about the existence of heaven and hell, but some of us know for sure that heaven is really there. We know because God gives us special moments with special people so we can feel a little bit of the joy we'll have when we get there. We know because He gives us brief, fleeting tastes of that kind of perfect security, that feeling of absolute safety and calm, every time we join Him at His Holy Table.

We know because Jesus tells us so. And He promises to save a spot there for us.

My little piece of peace ☺ on that vacation was tiny and brief, but I will always think of it when I need a bit of a refresh. A reminder of the good things to come.

"We have patrolled the earth, and behold, all the earth remains at rest."

ZECHARIAH 1:11

mansion

There are magazines that are totally devoted to peeking into the homes of other people. You can see their kitchens, cabinets open. Living rooms, including the books they read clearly sitting on the shelves. Or, in some baffling cases though, the homes completely devoid of books. Really? There isn't one person in their family who *reads?* Those are the homes that always throw me for a loop. My point is that nothing is held back in these displays, including the interior of their closets. The reader, one hopes, is completely aware that those homes can't possibly always look like that. They're staged for the photos and every single piece of lint and cat hair has been removed, and fresh flowers are made to appear in every bathroom. If you are the kind of person who really does have fresh flowers in every bathroom every day, call me. We need to talk.

So many people I know want one of those homes for their very own. When we take drives through really beautiful neighborhoods, my kids and I will often comment with awe about some of the houses we see there. One of my kids recently posed this question: "Do you want that house, Mommy? You said you think it's pretty." It made me laugh right out loud. "Absolutely not!" I replied.

Here's the situation; unless that kind of house comes with a housekeeper and a full maintenance crew, we should never have it. First of all, I'm pretty sure I would lose at least one kid in one of the massive wings or on one of the levels of such a house. And who can clean that much square footage? I lived in a house the size of some garages for a time, and I struggled with cleanliness in that tiny place, so I can't imagine keeping up with four levels, multi-car garage, and a solarium. Finding time to keep that yard pretty and those squiggly shaped bushes must be a challenge unto itself. I have three trees and a tomato garden, and I feel like I should get some sort of botany trophy just for that. (Now that I've said that, I think one of the trees might be dead; no trophy for me.)

It's like that for so many things I've desired in the past. Maybe you can relate:

> Ooooohhhhhhh! I really want that
> thing. I am so jealous that she has those,

that he just bought this, that they just
did that, etc. I want want want want
want, and why can't I have?

For me, I've learned that the simple answer is a
frank and honest one: I can't have because I couldn't
handle it. Case in point: I've wanted a corvette since
I was three, but I know I'll never have one. I'd kill
myself driving too fast—just letting you know right
now. At least that's what my dad said at the premise
of his three-year-old daughter (me) having such a fine
automobile. I'd like a light saber too, but the reason
I shouldn't have one needs no explanation.

So here's the thing: we will always struggle with
wanting to have things that we see. I'm pretty sure
it's in our human nature to have that desire. In some
ways, it helps us work hard to try to acquire things
that do benefit us and to appreciate them when we
get them. But keep in mind that some things simply
aren't meant for us. Our desire for more stuff is just
one of the ways that our enemy whispers in our ear
to distract us from the good gifts that God gives us
every day. It's how he convinces us to be dissatisfied
with how God provides for us. We won't have a maid,
we might drive too fast in that sports car, and light
sabers would cut all of our furniture in half.

But we do have everything that God knows is good for us. Everything. Even if pictures of it never make it into the pages of a magazine.

Now, if I can just get myself to stop coveting shoes. . . .

I coveted no one's silver or gold or apparel.

ACTS 20:33

amnesty

In 1863, an amazing thing happened right here in the United States of America. A very tender promise was made to the Confederate military. If they signed a statement, they could just go home to their families as free men. No punishment, no vengeance, no shame. It was a generous act of forgiveness. (Note that POWs experienced a delay in their release because they weren't free to go on the exact date of the signing.) Here are the words of that agreement, suggested by President Lincoln but penned by General Grant:

> "I, (repeat full name), do solemnly swear, in the presence of almighty God, that I will henceforth faithfully support, protect, and defend the Constitution of the United States, and the Union of the States thereunder; and that I will, in like manner, abide by and faithfully support all Acts of Congress passed during the existing rebellion with reference to slaves, so long and so

far as not repealed, modified, or held
void by Congress, or by the decision
of the Supreme Court; and that I will,
in like manner, abide by and faithfully
support all proclamations of the President made during the existing rebel-
lion having reference to slaves, so long
and so far as not modified or declared
void by decision of the Supreme Court,
so help me God."

This statement, the thing behind this act of
forgiveness, is, to the best of my research, an unusual
thing. An entire army of dissenters was invited to re-
join the rest of the nation it had previously rejected.
To adopt a new unity. To work, to struggle through
the difficulties that would direct all eyes toward the
hope for a better future for all. This new idea wasn't
a complete destruction of the entire southern region
(although the staunchest of that region's residents at
that time were hard-pressed to agree), but a plea to
work toward the end of that horrible, horrible war,
toward a national unity.

The loss of life in that war was soul-rending,
the trauma left scars on the very soil of this nation
that are visible still today. I am as moved when I look
on the graves of the victims of that conflict as I am
when I pay respect to soldiers lost in current wars.

So I call this agreement "tender" for a very deliberate reason. That war was so bitter, so cruel, so terrible that only a word like *tender* captures the nature of that gesture of freedom and forgiveness extended to the Confederates.

Savagery still exists in every war. Not just in conflicts between nations, but in our homes, families, work places, and even the church. There are savage wars within each of us too. Private wars. Personal conflicts. Long skirmishes and terrible battles in our minds and hearts.

We all struggle with so many conflicts, so many private wars, that I think we need an amnesty oath of our own. As veterans and casualties of our private wars, we need soothing, forgiveness, healing. And you know where that comes from, right?

When we call an end to the cruel battles that our enemy creates for us, we can drop our weapons—all that emotion that we wear like armor and wield like swords—and walk away from our private wars. Walk toward the One who hears our admission of guilt and tenderly promises forgiveness; the One who offers the peace that passes understanding and the promise of a perfect future of unity with Him. No punishment. No vengeance. No shame.

My prayer is that if we give ourselves that kind of amnesty, then we can offer one another a little olive branch too. For Jesus' sake.

"The LORD lift up His countenance upon you and give you peace.""

NUMBERS 6:25–27

Photo by Jeff Caso

ABOUT THE AUTHOR

Heidi (Staib) Floyd was born in a small town in Illinois and has always known the world as a fascinating and wonderful place. A lover of history and a perpetual student of faith, Heidi relishes the opportunity to discuss either at any time. Her faith has been omnipresent in her life, but she was given a wonderful example of a life lived in faith by her mother, Roberta, who passed away from breast cancer at a tragically young age. No matter the situation, Heidi looks to find the brightest possible part and focuses squarely on that hope. Her simple messages of compassion, hope and perseverance in the face of everyday challenges have been requested in print for several years, and she is now proud but terrified to present them to the public. ☺

Heidi attended Concordia College in Ann Arbor, Michigan, and is married to Stuart Floyd. They reside in Warsaw, Indiana, where he is a pastor at Redeemer Lutheran Church. They have four beautiful children who give them more joy than they had ever considered possible, true blessings every single day.